Presented to:

10 Commandments of Effective Worship Leading

Also by Ted Shuttlesworth Jr.

*A Complete Guide to Biblical Fasting:
Master the Habit that Provokes God's Favor*

The 21-Day Fast Field Guide

*Further Faster: How to Accelerate Your Purpose
Through the Force of Impartation*

*Unhang Your Harp: How Praise Opens the Door
to Every Blessing God Has Provided for You*

Blood on the Door: The Protective Power of Covenant

*Praise. Laugh. Repeat.: Living in the Power
of Overwhelming Joy*

*Praise. Laugh. Repeat. Devotional:
A 40-Day Journey to Overwhelming Joy*

(Also available on Apple Books and Amazon Kindle)

10 Commandments of Effective Worship Leading

AVOID COMMON MISTAKES,

DEVELOP YOUR GIFT,

& BUILD A STRONG TEAM

Ted Shuttlesworth Jr.

MIRACLE WORD
PUBLISHING

© 2024 by Ted Shuttlesworth Jr.

All rights reserved. No portion of this book may be reproduced, stored in a retrieval system, or transmitted in any form or by any means—electronic, mechanical, photocopy, recording, scanning, or other—except for brief quotations in critical reviews or articles, without the prior written permission of the publisher.

Published in Virginia Beach, Virginia by Miracle Word Publishing.

Miracle Word titles may be purchased in bulk for educational, business, fundraising, or sales promotional use. For information, please e-mail info@miracleword.com

Scripture quotations marked (NLT) are taken from the Holy Bible, New Living Translation, copyright ©1996, 2004, 2015 by Tyndale House Foundation. Used by permission of Tyndale House Publishers, Carol Stream, Illinois 60188. All rights reserved.

Scripture quotations marked NKJV are from the NEW KING JAMES VERSION. © 1982 by Thomas Nelson, Inc. Used by permission. All rights reserved.

Scripture quotations are from the ESV® Bible (The Holy Bible, English Standard Version®), copyright © 2001 by Crossway, a publishing ministry of Good News Publishers. Used by permission. All rights reserved.

Scripture quotations marked HCSB are taken from the Holman Christian Standard Bible®, Copyright © 1999, 2000, 2002, 2003, 2009 by Holman Bible Publishers. Used by permission. Holman Christian Standard Bible®, Holman CSB®, and HCSB® are federally registered trademarks of Holman Bible Publishers.

Scripture quotations taken from the Amplified® Bible (AMPC), Copyright © 1954, 1958, 1962, 1964, 1965, 1987 by The Lockman Foundation
Used by permission. lockman.org

All uppercase and italicized text in verses of Scripture are added by the author for the purpose of emphasis.

ISBN 978-1-7349962-8-9

Printed in the United States of America

For the Worshipers.

CONTENTS

GET SOME JOY
PAGE ONE

DESTROY THE EGOMANIAC
PAGE FIFTEEN

DEDICATE YOUR GIFT TO GOD
PAGE TWENTY-SEVEN

BE A PERSON OF PRAYER
PAGE THIRTY-NINE

REMEMBER WHO'S IN THE ROOM
PAGE FORTY-NINE

HAVE SOMETHING TO SAY
PAGE FIFTY-NINE

NO UNSCRIPTURAL SONGS
PAGE SIXTY-NINE

MASTER TRANSITIONS
PAGE SEVENTY-NINE

FOLLOW THE LEADER
PAGE NINETY-ONE

STEADILY IMPROVE YOUR GIFT
PAGE ONE HUNDRED FIVE

Joy is magnetic. It might be the most important attribute (other than holiness) that a worshiper can have. Activate it!

— Pastor Ted

COMMANDMENT ONE
GET SOME JOY!

I was standing in the front row of the church, and I was mad enough to cuss. I didn't, though. Thank God for self-control. It was the first night of a revival, and I was about to preach. However, the praise and worship leader sabotaged the service before I could get the microphone.

"How many know life is hard?" He droned, slowly strumming his acoustic guitar. "I'm sure all of us have been through hell this week. I know many of us are struggling."

What part of this train wreck is praise or worship? I wondered. Then, he dropped it on us—the cry voice.

You're familiar with the religious cry voice. It's somewhere between a wail and a moan (and a long way from God's presence). It's not actually crying. It's fake. Like lousy acting in a community college theater class. (No offense if you're currently enrolled in one.)

"Oh, God! We're so unworrrrrthy!" He held that one out for effect. I couldn't take much more of this. He continued, and all I wanted was to body slam him—in love, of course.

God is the object of our praise and worship. It's never about us. His greatness, glory, power, and majesty should always be the central focus.

I knew that I would have to resurrect this service soon with the Holy Spirit's help. Unfortunately, situations like this would happen often in the early stages of my traveling ministry.

Though I wished I could flow straight into ministering to people after the praise and worship, this type of poorly executed, soul-driven worship forced me to compartmentalize the services in my mind.

I'd let the worship team do their part, and then when I took the microphone, it was like starting the service from scratch.

I'd often walk straight to the keyboard and sing and play until I felt the anointing to preach.

This thought process isn't based on pride. There is a proper and improper way to approach God and worship him. If you do it improperly, it's not only displeasing to God, but you also fail to prepare the hearts of those about to receive God's Word.

This chapter will explain your important responsibility as a praise and worship leader. Trust me; praise and worship isn't just a buffer at the beginning of the service to allow the late crowd to arrive before the sermon starts.

Beginning with praise and worship is also not just about church tradition. It's far more than that.

WHAT THE DEVIL DOESN'T WANT YOU TO KNOW

When we view the purpose of praise and worship from a biblical perspective, we realize the vast importance of doing it—and doing it right.

According to Jesus' parable of the sower, there are four different types of ground. He explains that the various types of "ground" represent the types of people who hear God's Word.

The first group is people who don't understand the Word when they hear it. The Pastor's job is to preach it clearly so they can understand.

Second, some people detach from the Word when they encounter persecution because their roots aren't deep. This departure is a discipleship problem.

However, the third type of person that Jesus deals with is the type of person you will encounter the most as a worship leader. These are the people who represent "thorny ground."

Those whom Jesus described as thorny ground hear the Word but cannot produce fruit because the worries of life and the lure of wealth overtake them. (See Matthew 13:18-23.)

One translation refers to the worries of life as the "cares of this world." The enemy uses what's going on in the world to bring worry, anxiety, and heaviness into a person's life so they can't properly receive God's Word.

We see a perfect example of this principle when Jesus called Peter out of the boat to walk on water. When Peter acted on that word from Jesus, it empowered him to do something supernatural.

However, on his way to Jesus, he averted his eyes and began focusing on the enormous waves surrounding him. Once he took his eyes off of the Word and put them on the waves, he began to sink.

That's what happens. When we stop focusing on God's Word and begin focusing on what's happening in the world, we can't produce fruit and accomplish our God-given purpose.

Most people in the congregation have experienced

negativity all week long. Unless they've disciplined themselves to renew their minds daily, they come into church with worry, anxiety, and heaviness weighing on their spirits.

They're in the worst possible position to receive God's Word. God knew this would happen and created a solution ahead of time.

THE PRAISE ANTIDOTE

The moment we begin praising God, it activates his presence. He's enthroned on our praises (Psalm 22:3). Although God is omnipresent, not every person constantly benefits from his presence.

As the author of Hebrews wrote, God only rewards those who actively seek him (Hebrews 11:6). By praising God, we truly seek him, which activates his presence in our lives.

What takes place as we praise him is the antidote for heaviness and anxiety. Look what David wrote:

> You make known to me the path of life;
> in your presence there is fullness of joy; at
> your right hand are pleasures forevermore.
> Psalm 16:11 ESV

Properly focused praise activates God's presence and gives us access to overwhelming joy! When that happens, heaviness and anxiety have to go. David described it as "fullness of joy." I have no room for anything else if I'm full of joy.

It's not circular reasoning to say we should joyfully praise him to access his presence and receive joy. Don't forget the context of what I'm teaching: *those in the congregation* need to receive this joy so that their hearts are ready to receive God's Word.

However, you are the leader. That means you should already be carrying overwhelming joy! You cannot lead someone somewhere that you've never been. You cannot give what you don't have.

The devil would love to fight against a weak church, but as Nehemiah wrote, the joy of the Lord is our strength (Nehemiah 8:10). As we walk in joy, we're walking in strength.

Furthermore, Isaiah prophesied that salvation would be available to Israel. He told them that joy would be the element with which they would draw water from the wells of their salvation (Isaiah 12:3).

Your salvation contains wells that God filled with his blessings. Joy is the bucket that allows you to draw water from those wells. Can you see how vital the element of joy is? It's a must. If the devil can deceive you into surrendering your bucket, your wells will remain inaccessible.

Joy must be a significant element of your praise and worship. Later, I'll give you practical tips so you can implement all of these principles.

THE MULTIDIMENSIONAL POWER OF JOY

It's essential to remember that supernatural joy is an accelerant. Not only does it produce strength, but it's also medicine for your body.

> A joyful heart is good medicine, but a crushed spirit dries up the bones.
>
> Proverbs 17:22 ESV

According to the Mayo Clinic, your body releases endorphins—the "feel good hormone"—when you laugh.[1] God designed your body to respond to joy.

God created joy as a vehicle for victory. That's why we're commanded to rejoice throughout Scripture.

> Rejoice in the Lord always; again I will say, rejoice.
>
> Philippians 4:4 ESV

To rejoice is to show great joy or delight. It doesn't matter whether or not someone feels happy; Scripture commands every Christian to exhibit boundless joy consistently.

Engaging in proper praise daily is one way to ensure that you'll exhibit great joy in your life with Christ. Let me share a basic mistake many praise and worship leaders make.

INSUFFICIENT PRAISE

In modern church services, we often define praise songs as the faster, more intense songs in our set, while we also refer to slower ballads as worship songs.

The discussion of biblical praise and worship requires a deeper study and more complex answers, but for the sake of this section, I'll use the common definition.

The upbeat, joyful music we call praise is often neglected in many churches. Some have removed it altogether, which is a major mistake.

God has a system by which we approach him. The Lord commanded even his Old Testament people to approach his temple in a specific way. Jesus is the King of kings. We should take care to interact with him properly.

> Enter his gates with thanksgiving, and his courts with praise! Give thanks to him; bless his name!
>
> Psalm 100:4 ESV

The temple consisted of the outer court, the inner court, and the holy of holies—a place only the high priest could reverently enter. Those three places represent thanksgiving, praise, and worship.

Until you've sufficiently praised God, you're not qualified to worship him.

When I first started as a praise and worship leader, I drove fifteen hours round trip every weekend to lead worship.

During those drives, I would praise, worship, and pray in the Spirit the entire trip. I was prepping myself for the Friday night service.

One weekend, I made a huge mistake that I've never made again. I came into the service after having praised God for seven straight hours, and as a result, I had a very different mindset than those who came into church after a long workday.

I started the service by having everyone lift their hands, and I began to worship the Lord slowly. *That's where I was.* However, as the leader, I should have known that's not where they were. The congregation just stood and stared at me. We hadn't sufficiently praised God and weren't prepared to worship him.

The service droned on and lacked joy. Rather than being an intimate and powerful time of worship, it felt heavy and dead.

I should have joyfully praised God and properly led his people into his presence. Victory has a very specific sound—it sounds like joy.

THE SOUND OF VICTORY

I enjoy watching soccer. Normally, the scores aren't very high. It's one of the only sports where a match can end in a tie.

Teams only score a few goals throughout the match, so it's a big deal when one does happen. Because it is, there are significant celebrations afterward.

Sometimes, a player may take off his jersey and run around the field; other times, there are preplanned celebrations between the goal scorer and his teammates while the stadium erupts in deafening screams.

I prefer watching highlights on one of the Spanish-speaking channels because the commentary is far more emotional.

Though I can't understand what they're saying, I can feel the tension and excitement building in their voices. Finally, when a goal is scored, it's the most extravagant commentary celebration you've ever heard.

After a big breath, the commentator will scream, "Goal," and hold it out for about twenty seconds. It's quite different from listening to the British commentary. Victory has a distinct sound.

It's so much better listening to the commentary that exudes the most joy and excitement. Why? Because it *imparts* joy and excitement. Why would I, a non-Spanish speaker, listen to it over English commentary? Because of how it makes me feel about the match.

The same is true as you lead praise and worship. You can impart joy simply by how you present what you're doing. Are you not excited to worship? No one else will be either. True leaders inspire.

> So David went and brought up the ark of God from the house of Obed-edom to the city of David with rejoicing . . . And David danced before the Lord with all his might . . . So David and all the house of Israel brought up the ark of the Lord with shouting and with the sound of the horn.
>
> 2 Samuel 6:12, 13-14 ESV

The rejoicing began with David and finished with the entire house of Israel rejoicing with him. Joy is contagious and should always define an effective worship leader's life.

Never make the mistake of losing your joy. I believe every service should begin with joyful praise and, unless it would be inappropriate for the context of the service, finish with joyful praise. Be a conduit of joy.

NOTES

1. Mayo Clinic Staff. "Stress Relief from Laughter? It's No Joke." Mayo Clinic, Mayo Foundation for Medical Education and Research, 22 Sept. 2023, https://www.mayoclinic.org/healthy-lifestyle/stress-management/in-depth/stress-relief/art-20044456.

Checklist

(1) Encourage yourself and stimulate your joy by praying in the Spirit on a daily basis (1 Corinthians 14:4).

(2) Generate supernatural joy by filling yourself with a steady diet of God's Word (Jeremiah 15:16).

(3) Guard your heart from heaviness and anxiety by filtering what you allow yourself to see and hear. Even if you get a bad report, believe God's Word instead (Philippians 4:8).

(4) When leading worship, focus on the greatness of God. Don't draw attention to natural problems. Instead, talk about God's unlimited abilities (Psalm 150).

(5) On days when you're leading worship, guard yourself from interactions that would anger or frustrate you. The enemy knows how to send people to irritate your spirit in order to hinder your purpose. Jealously guard your peace and joy.

PRIDE MAKES GOD YOUR OPPONENT.

COMMANDMENT TWO
DESTROY THE EGOMANIAC

I glanced at the back doors and shook my head in disappointment again for about the thousandth time. I looked down at my watch.

9:02 am.

The band and I were finishing our Sunday morning rehearsal, and our bass player was nowhere to be found. We'd all been at the church since 8:00 am, right on time. Somehow, he was late again.

I was frustrated. This had become a pattern. My drummer lived an hour away from the church and was always on time. However, my bass player lived five minutes away and was *never* on time.

As a band member, being on time didn't mean showing up a few minutes before church started at

10:00 am; it meant 8:00 am with everyone else. I was tired of this nonsense. Every Sunday was the same. Everyone else on the team would be punctual and ready to go.

After rehearsals, we'd wait for our bass player. He wouldn't show up. Finally, it would be time for service to start, and we couldn't wait any longer. I'd welcome the congregation and begin praise and worship.

Then, around 10:07 am, our bass player would burst into the back door with his guitar strapped on. He'd stand by the sound booth and motion to me pointing at himself and then to the platform. His message was plain.

Do you want me to come up and play?

To be clear, this would never have happened today. However, I was only nineteen and fresh out of Bible school. I'd never led a team before and was still learning how to navigate personalities and boundaries so I could lead with excellence.

On this specific Sunday, I was in the same position again. We began the service, and, like always, our bass player walked in the door holding his guitar.

Something had to change.

After we finished, I told the band to meet me in one of the church's offices. It was time for a meeting. Pride was destroying our unity and strength.

THE POISON THAT KILLS PURPOSE

In that room, with the band surrounding me, I laid out a very uncomfortable truth. Our bass player was late every Sunday, not because he was busy, had young children, lived too far away, or was a poor manager of his time.

He was late because he was egotistical, selfish, and proud. You might not have thought this was true if you had met him. He was a very nice guy.

However, actions speak much louder than words.

He was constantly late and dishonored his fellow band members and the Lord because he was filled with pride.

In his mind, the rules didn't apply to him. He acted like what was mandatory for everyone else was a suggestion for him, and he proved that by consistently shirking his responsibilities.

Needless to say, we got another bass player. When we did, everything changed. Even our worship services were more anointed. Unity was back.

After traveling full-time for more than twenty years, I've met many musicians and singers. Unfortunately, many of them have large egos and want to be treated like rock stars. I quickly decided to distance myself from anyone like that. I wanted to surround myself with humble people. I don't care how much talent someone has if their attitude is wrong.

I would rather work with someone humble, who has 60% of the talent, than with the most talented person, who is filled with pride.

Don't miss this—God hates pride.

He hates it so much that he actively works against people who live pridefully. This is so important that the apostles James and Peter quote the Greek version of Proverbs 3:34.

> But he gives more grace. Therefore it says, "God opposes the proud but gives grace to the humble."
>
> James 4:6 ESV

Think about how intense that truth is. God hates pride so much that he opposes the proud. Allowing pride to rule your life makes God your opponent.

Understanding this principle makes it easy to see why pride is so destructive. If God is against you, how can you succeed?

> Pride goes before destruction, and a haughty spirit before a fall.
>
> Proverbs 16:18 ESV

The good news is that the opposite is also true. If you're humble and meek, God is actively working to promote you.

> Humble yourselves, therefore, under the mighty hand of God so that at the proper time he may exalt you,
>
> 1 Peter 5:6 ESV

As James wrote, God gives grace to the humble. Proverbs 3:34 says that he releases favor to those who are humble.

Think about it this way: humility is a magnet that attracts God's favor. There is no limit to how high God can lift you when you eliminate all pride from your life and walk humbly before him.

You should notice something significant about the verse above. Peter wrote, "Humble yourselves." It's our responsibility to resist the natural urge to be prideful and put ourselves in a place of humility.

CELEBRITY SYNDROME

Years ago, a friend of mine decided to host a worship conference at his church and invited the world's most well-known Christian artists.

Of course, the artists immediately sent him their lists of demands and requirements. These "riders" can include anything from the type of bottled water the artist prefers to the type of toilet paper they want in their hotel room and green room. (Yes, that's real.)

The artist who would headline the conference sent his financial demands. He wanted a cashier's check for $16,000.

On the day of the conference, the artist arrived at the church, and the Pastor, excited to have him there, went outside to greet him.

The artist refused to get out of the car. He looked at the Pastor and said, "I will not sing one note until I get my $16,000."

This destructive celebrity mentality has seeped into the body of Christ. It's self-focused instead of Christ-focused, and it ignores an important principle.

> I am the vine; you are the branches. Whoever abides in me and I in him, he it is that bears much fruit, for apart from me you can do nothing.
>
> John 15:5 ESV

It's one thing to have skill; it's another thing to be anointed. Ideally, you want to have both. However,

I've been to church services where those leading worship weren't the most talented singers or musicians, but God mightily anointed them. As they praised God, people were healed and delivered.

I've been to Broadway shows that employ the most professional singers and musicians. The performances are superb, but no one is healed.

I've even been to churches that hire studio musicians to lead the praise and worship, but the anointing isn't there. If I had to choose, I'd rather be anointed than talented. Thank God we don't have to choose.

Remember, if it's about you, it's not about God. There can only be one focus.

THE UNLIKELY PROMOTION

Imagine being born as a slave and then being placed in charge of the kingdom into which you were born. That sounds like a classic rags-to-riches story: the unlikely hero and the underdog.

That's precisely what happened to Moses. Something was different about him. There was an element of his life that drew upon God's favor — his meekness.

It seems as though the level of Moses' meekness determined the level of greatness God could release to him. Let's compare two revealing passages.

> Now the man Moses was very meek, more than all people who were on the face of the earth.
>
> Numbers 12:3 ESV

How amazing is that? There was no one on the earth more humble than Moses. Meekness was truly the key to his greatness. His meekness gives us insight into how God used him so powerfully.

> And the LORD gave the people favor in the sight of the Egyptians. Moreover, the man Moses was very great in the land of Egypt, in the sight of Pharaoh's servants and in the sight of the people.
>
> Exodus 11:3 ESV

The meekest man became the greatest man. That's because God exalts the humble (1 Peter 5:6). Jesus also taught that meekness was the key to supernatural inheritance (Matthew 5:5).

If you want God to use you mightily in any area of ministry, you have to make up your mind that pride will never be a part of your life. Be watchful, and fight to keep it far away from you. There's nothing Satan would like more than to trap you in pride.

THE BEST DEFINITION OF HUMILITY

There's no reason to make humility complicated. It's simple. The common definition of humility is "a modest or low view of one's importance."

However, I want to give you a scriptural definition. Biblical humility acknowledges that God's ways are higher than yours, which produces obedience. God revealed this in the book of Isaiah.

> For as the heavens are higher than the earth, so are my ways higher than your ways and my thoughts than your thoughts.
> Isaiah 55:9 ESV

Simply put, biblical humility is obedience to God's Word. When we disobey God's commands, we're saying our ways are higher than his. However, obedience is proof that we know his ways are higher.

Obedience is proof of love and qualification for God's manifested power in our lives. Though that might be an unpopular thought in the modern church, John revealed this fact in his Gospel.

Talk is cheap. Anyone can say they love God, but in John 14, Jesus defined what it looks like when someone truly loves him.

> Whoever has my commandments and keeps them, he it is who loves me. And he who loves me will be loved by my Father, and I will love him and manifest myself to him.
>
> John 14:21 ESV

This is humility. As you can see, God blesses meekness and only pours his favor out on those who meet the conditions. Remember, he's only a rewarder of those who genuinely seek him (Hebrews 11:6).

As you eliminate all pride from your life and humble yourself before the Lord, expect his powerful blessings to follow you as you worship and praise him. Make a rule: no egos on the team.

(1) Examine yourself daily. Have you made obeying God's Word a priority? Have you subdued your carnal nature? (1 Corinthians 9:27).

(2) Examine your team. Are there divas? Is it time to have a meeting about focused humility?

(3) Like my old bass player, is there anyone who refuses to change and needs to be removed from the team?

(4) Have you felt yourself begin to slack in your dedication to your gift or purpose?

(5) Is there anything you can do today to humble yourself further before the Lord?

A DEDICATED GIFT WILL ALWAYS BE A DYNAMIC GIFT.

COMMANDMENT THREE
DEDICATE YOUR GIFT TO GOD

In my teens, my father traveled and ministered with Evangelist R.W. Schambach, a mighty revivalist.

I loved the powerful Pentecostal praise and worship in his tent meetings. Upbeat, happy, deliverance music that you could dance to. I loved listening to the drums, bass, keyboard, and my favorite, the B3 Hammond organ and Leslie speaker.

(Many Pentecostals might argue that you can't even have a proper Holy Ghost service without a Hammond organ in the room.)

Every night, I would stand in the front row and dance through the praise and worship service. When I was bolder, I crept around the back of the platform, stood next to the edge, and watched the organist play.

I'm unsure how, but I eventually found a seat on the bench next to the organist each night. I would watch in amazement at how "Wild" Willie Isaac (the organist) and Lance Palmer (the keyboardist and worship leader) would play their instruments.

I loved it, and I wanted to play like they did. Brother Schambach would come out on the platform every night, see me sitting there, and smile.

In the final meeting of each ten-day tent crusade, he would hold a children's blessing service.

In one of those services, as I walked through the prayer line with thousands of others, Brother Schambach stopped and laid his hands on me.

He prayed that the anointing would come upon my life from that night to play and sing the same kind of Pentecostal music I loved so much.

Looking back, I realize now that after he laid hands on me, the Spirit of the Lord came mightily upon me from that day forward. (See 1 Samuel 16:13.)

MY DEDICATION VOW TO GOD

Soon after, as I learned more about playing the keyboard, I made a vow to God. I told him that if he would anoint and use me to praise and worship, I would only ever use my gifts for his kingdom. I promised I'd never use it in cafes, bars, or clubs to make money. I vowed never to go on tour and play with secular artists. My gifts belong to the Lord.

As a result, I've experienced God's power and seen supernatural things take place through praise and worship.

One example took place as I was speaking at a church near Mount Airy, North Carolina. Sunday morning, I announced that I would pray for those needing healing during the evening service.

That night, people came who needed a touch from the Lord. As I often do before preaching, I sat at the keyboard and began playing. I led the congregation in singing hymns about the blood of Jesus.

After I preached, I asked everyone who needed prayer to come to the altar. I then went down the line, laying hands on each person.

Finally, I came to an older man and his wife. He was standing there with a big smile on his face.

"What do you need God to do for you?" I asked.

"I came here tonight believing God would open my deaf ear," he replied. "But at the beginning of the service, as you were playing and we were all singing, my ear popped open!"

Nobody needed to pray for the man. As we praised and worshiped, God released healing power that opened the man's deaf ear. Praise and worship activate God's presence, and he is the healer. Again, there's a difference between talent and anointing. It's the anointing that sets people free.

EMPTYING AN ITALIAN BAR

I was in Venice, Italy, with my family, staying at a beautiful hotel. We spent the entire day walking around the city, admiring the architecture, and seeing the sights.

When we returned to the hotel later that night, I noticed that the ballroom and bar were packed with people dressed in evening wear. It looked like a scene from a James Bond movie.

I glanced across the marble-floored ballroom and saw a baby grand piano. Maybe it's just me, but as a pianist, seeing a grand piano and not playing it is challenging. This is probably a common problem because the keyboards are usually locked and inaccessible.

I couldn't help myself. Though I was sweaty from being out all day and wearing my informal, casual clothes, I entered the ballroom and walked across the marble floor toward the piano.

The people wearing tuxedos and evening gowns standing at the bar talking and laughing glanced at me as I approached. I looked out of place in that room.

I sat down, and to my surprise, the hotel hadn't locked the piano. The lid was already up. I knew that the acoustics would be excellent in that marble ballroom.

I began to play (not sing) songs about the blood of Jesus. I could immediately feel the anointing of the Holy Spirit in that room.

I played "jazzed up" versions of the hymns, so my playing didn't seem out of place in that setting. However, you could feel everything change as the anointing began to fill the room.

People gathered their belongings and left the bar one by one. I imagine it's hard to hook up and make plans to have sex with someone who's not your wife while songs about the blood of Jesus are playing in the background. The anointing always brings conviction to those who need it.

After about twenty minutes, the formerly packed bar was empty, and only an elderly couple that was eating dinner remained. I laughed when they turned and asked me if I knew *Fly Me to the Moon*.

When you dedicate your gift to God it is consecrated and becomes holy rather than common. Your gift carries God's presence.

COVENANT CONSECRATION

There's something about consecrating yourself to God that allows him to use you mightily. Dedicating your gifts to him is a form of consecration.

This was true even in the Old Testament. As God's people approached Jericho, they needed a miracle to cross the Jordan River. Look at this instruction:

> Then Joshua said to the people, "Consecrate yourselves, for tomorrow the LORD will do wonders among you."
>
> Joshua 3:5 ESV

Consecration positions you to be a powerful vessel for God to use in his kingdom. It's imperative to understand that God doesn't consecrate us. We have a responsibility to consecrate ourselves.

The apostle Paul was Timothy's spiritual father. Paul was training Timothy to reach his God-given potential. He wrote and gave Timothy this instruction:

> In a wealthy home some utensils are made of gold and silver, and some are made of wood and clay. The expensive utensils are used for special occasions, and the cheap

> ones are for everyday use. If you keep yourself pure, you will be a special utensil for honorable use. Your life will be clean, and you will be ready for the Master to use you for every good work.
>
> 2 Timothy 2:20-21 NLT

Dedicating your gift to God keeps it pure. People think I'm crazy when I say that if an internationally known secular artist called me and asked me to play the keyboard on their tour, I'd refuse.

"You'd have such an open door to minister," some people say. At what cost? Compromising my gift? Do I want to be on stage every night playing songs that objectify women or have foul language? Obviously not. My gifts are reserved for the Lord.

I once knew a very talented praise and worship leader. He even wrote songs that blessed me. One year, I returned to the church where he had been the music director, but he was gone. They had replaced him with someone else. When I asked where he was, they told me they had to let him go.

On Saturday evenings, he would come to the church and break down the music equipment. Then, he and his friends would play at multiple clubs or bars on Saturday nights to make extra money.

They would set the equipment back in the church before Sunday service and then lead worship. You cannot be flippant with your gift and expect God to use you mightily.

TWO MIRACLES IN ONE

It was the final night of the West Virginia Campmeeting—an annual spring revival hosted by my father—and we were in the middle of praise and worship.

The B3 Hammond organ was screaming in true Pentecostal fashion as we sang one of my favorite songs: Funeral Plans. You might think that's an odd name for a praise and worship song, but the lyrics are a powerful declaration of dedication to the Spirit.

When I die, let me die speaking in tongues.

People shouted, clapped, and danced in that atmosphere of faith and Holy Ghost power.

Suddenly, a man began to shout, dropped his crutches, and took off running around the church.

Although his legs had been crippled for some time after a car accident, as we were praising God, the Holy Spirit touched him, and he was instantly healed.

Just in front of him stood a man who was deaf in one ear and blind in one eye due to the adverse effects of a previous surgery.

At the exact moment the Lord healed the crippled man's legs, this man's deaf ear began to hear, and his blind eye opened.

He began jumping up and down, and you could hear him shouting, "I can see! I can hear!"

Notice that no one laid hands on these men. The message hadn't even been preached yet. God released his healing power as we praised him.

I previously included this story in a book I wrote entitled *Unhang Your Harp*, in which I reveal how praise opens the door to every blessing God has provided for you. If you're a worshiper, I highly recommend obtaining a copy of that book.

SAMSON SYNDROME

I'm sure you know Samson's story from the book of Judges. If you've not studied it closely, you may not know that he made a Nazirite Vow. The word "Nazirite" means one who is separated or consecrated.

One of the terms of the vow was that he could never cut his hair. His long hair was one of the signs of his separation and consecration to God.

As long as Samson's hair was untouched, God empowered him, and he performed exploits for Israel. However, when Delilah finally discovered his secret, she had someone shave his head while Samson was sleeping, and he lost his power. He was taken captive by the Philistines and humiliated by those he used to dominate.

I want you to see that although Samson didn't shave his head, he refused to separate himself from someone working against his purpose.

This wasn't the first incident he'd had with Delilah. Every time he gave her a false secret of his power, she exploited it. He should have known.

What can you take away from this story? Refuse to compromise your gifts or allow others to convince you to use your gifts for a secular purpose.

Be a "vessel of gold," and let God use you to do mighty things in his kingdom.

> **THE ENEMY WILL SEND PEOPLE WHO TRY TO COMPROMISE YOUR GIFT.**

(1) Have you made your own vow to God? What about your life lets God know that what he has given you is reserved for him?

(2) Have you been flippant with your gifts in the past? What can you change today that shows God you'll honor him with what he's placed in your life?

(3) Have you ever seen God use your praise and worship to bring about supernatural things? If not, pray and ask God to use you mightily. He will!

(4) Examine your life. Is there anyone around you with the same motives Delilah had?

(5) What conversations can you have to let those people know that you won't use your gifts for anything that doesn't glorify God?

"Much prayer, much power. Little prayer, little power. No prayer, no power."

— E.M. Bounds

COMMANDMENT FOUR
BE A PERSON OF PRAYER

Have you ever been in a church service and as the worship leader transitions between songs, he launches into a prayer that sounds like this:

"Father God, we just come to you now, Father God. We thank you, Father God, for your goodness, Father God. And we know, Father God, that you're here, Father God. We ask you, Father God, to just fill us up, Father God, until we overflow, Father God."

When someone prays publicly, it becomes very evident whether or not they pray privately. The lack of a personal prayer life often leaves your public prayers forced and awkward.

You're finally addressing someone you should have spoken with throughout the week but haven't talked to for a long time. As a result, you have to use filler words to give yourself extra time to figure out what you will say next.

How would it seem if you had everyday conversations like that?

"Chris, I just wanted to ask you, oh Chris, if you'd like to go to lunch, oh Chris. We could get Mexican, oh Chris. I'd like to just catch up, oh Chris. And I'd like to ask you right now, oh Chris, if you'd like to ride together, oh Chris."

They would look at you like you'd lost your mind.

You can tell when two people talk often. There's a familiarity as they speak. They laugh at the same things and have inside jokes.

The prompting to praise God and the power of your praise are byproducts of your personal prayer life because you develop a familiarity with God and his presence — which makes all the difference.

Familiarity brings comfort. Your familiarity with God's presence removes any anxiety about interacting with him because love drives the desire to seek his presence.

The Word of God tells us that perfect love drives out fear (1 John 4:18). Spending time in prayer allows you to experience the landscape of God's presence personally, which is extremely important as a worship leader.

YOU CAN'T TAKE SOMEONE SOMEWHERE YOU'VE NEVER BEEN

The term worship leader suggests that you guide people into a place of praise and worship. That means you must be familiar with the territory of meaningful, engaging worship and dynamic, breakthrough praise.

Imagine booking your first safari in the jungles of Africa. You finally land on the continent and drive out into the wilderness, ready to see dangerous animals you've never encountered before.

Finally, after traveling in the Jeep for over an hour, you ask your guide if you're getting close to the destination.

"I don't know," he replies. "This is my first time in Africa, as well."

He's completely unqualified to be your guide. He doesn't know the terrain. He's unfamiliar with the culture, and you'll likely end up lost.

That's what happens in many churches today. Leaders are not equipped to guide anyone into the presence of God because they also haven't been there. How can you lead someone somewhere that you've never been? You can't.

The best you can do in that situation is perform. Worship becomes a soulish concert. People end up watching the worship team and become completely disengaged. This is contrary to how Jesus instructed us to worship God.

> God is Spirit, and those who worship Him must worship in spirit and truth.
>
> John 4:24 NKJV

If I look across the crowd and people are standing with their hands on the back of the chair in front of them, sitting down, or just scrolling through Instagram, I'm failing as a worship leader.

As worship leaders, we must be anointed enough to bring God's presence into the room with us and then draw those who have come to church into the power of his presence.

We must access the spirit realm when we praise and worship God. Prayer and fasting are the keys that allow you to become familiar with the landscape of God's presence ahead of time.

One of the reasons God was able to use David in such a mighty way is that David's spirit was so sensitive to God's spirit.

When David arrived at the battlefield, Goliath was taunting Israel. David became grieved when he heard Goliath's blasphemy. As soon as he heard the way Goliath mocked the God of Israel, he immediately wanted to destroy him.

The other soldiers didn't have the same intense desire to destroy Goliath as David because they didn't have the same intense love for God.

David had spent many hours alone in the field praying, singing, playing his harp, and writing psalms. He had a close, personal relationship with God.

How did David know there was fullness of joy in God's presence? How did he know you could taste and see the Lord's goodness before reaching Heaven?

David could describe the wonderful benefits and attributes of God's presence because he had been there many times.

AN INTERACTIVE EXPERIENCE

This close relationship brought God's delivering presence into King Saul's court the moment David began playing his harp (1 Samuel 16:23).

Notice that prayer—and times of fasting—are interactive elements. They provoke God and release His power in your life. David's consistent dedication to the presence of God meant that he carried the power of God with him. Furthermore, he was aware of God's presence wherever he went.

> Where can I go to escape Your Spirit?
> Where can I flee from Your presence?
>
> Psalm 139:7 HCSB

The same was true for Christ. After forty days of fasting and prayer in the wilderness, he returned in the power of the Holy Spirit, and his ministry of signs and wonders began (Luke 4:14).

Christ's dedication to prayer and fasting allowed him to operate in miracle-working power daily.

He transferred this ability to his disciples so that they could perform the same level of miracles that he did. The only problem was that they had his power but lacked his dedication.

On one occasion, parents brought their son to be healed by the disciples. He was possessed by a demon spirit that often tried to kill him. The disciples tried unsuccessfully to heal the boy.

When Jesus heard about this, He rebuked them, quickly healed the boy, and cast the spirit out of him. The disciples were confused.

Later, they asked Jesus why they had no success in their attempts to cast that particular spirit out. Jesus answered them by comparing their dedication to his own.

> So he said to them, "This kind can come out by nothing but prayer and fasting."
>
> Mark 9:29 NKJV

We can clearly see that the disciples didn't have the same dedication to prayer as Jesus. As a result, although they received a direct impartation of power from Jesus, they couldn't fully activate it.

The level of power you release as a worshiper is connected to the amount of time you pray.

In Matthew chapter 26, Jesus led the disciples into a garden to pray. Once they had entered the garden, He went further and left them alone.

He returned an hour later and found them all asleep. He woke them, encouraged them to pray, and left them again. Afterward, he had to return and wake them up two more times.

It was the disciples' lack of prayer that short-circuited their power. I've often said that because Jesus completely yielded to the Father's will, if he hadn't heard his Father speaking through prayer, he would have been mute.

> . . . I do nothing on my own authority, but speak just as the Father taught me.
>
> John 8:28 ESV

Prayer makes Christianity an interactive experience. No other religion or false god can hear, answer, or do anything as a result of prayers. Only our God—who is alive—can interact with us through this powerful system.

I'm encouraging you to make prayer a daily priority. Like the first-century church, try to spend at least an hour praying each day. As you do, you'll notice a change in your ministry.

Become very familiar with God's presence, and you'll be able to quickly and successfully lead others there as well.

(1) What time-wasters can you remove from your life to spend more time in prayer?

(2) Do you have a method to capture the thoughts or ideas God gives you during prayer? If not, develop your own system.

(3) Take your worship goals and insert them directly into your prayer time. God wants your ministry to be as effective and dynamic as possible.

(4) Do you have Scriptures you're standing on as you pray? If not, create your own prayer points or download them from the Miracle Word app.

(5) Develop a system that eliminates all distractions for your prayer time. Prioritize it, and God will bless you for it.

The goal is not to simply lead worship; the goal is to lead people to Jesus —

COMMANDMENT FIVE
REMEMBER WHO'S IN THE ROOM

I was cringing so hard I thought I'd disintegrate. The worship leader had stopped singing to encourage us in our worship. He was preparing to throw some life experience at us and try to make an analogy that would draw us deeper into worship . . . he thought.

"When I come home after work each day, I have two little girls who have been waiting for me," he said. "When I walk in the door, they come running to cuddle up in my arms. All they want is for daddy to be their tickle monster."

Oh no.

I didn't know where this was going, but it wasn't going to be good. I underestimated how bad it would be. (I'm still recounting this story to you almost twenty-five years later. That's how scorched into my memory this is.) His next words made me want to disappear from the room.

"That's like our heavenly Father," he continued. "He just wants to be our tickle monster as we run into his arms."

Many years have passed since this happened, and I can still feel bile rising in my throat as I write this. Also, as a person who prays and talks to the Lord often, I can assure you that he has no desire to tickle you. Tickle monster . . . still shaking my head.

PLEASE DON'T MAKE THIS MISTAKE

As a worship leader, you must remember that there are almost always unsaved people in the crowd. Don't compromise the integrity of what the Holy Spirit is doing in them by saying cringy, awkward, or, for lack of a better word, dumb things.

I also won't sing some songs because I'm uncomfortable singing them. If I'm uncomfortable singing them, I can guarantee unsaved people are also.

Years ago, a popular song contained lyrics about laying back against Jesus' chest and breathing as you listened to his heartbeat.

Yeah, no. I'm not singing that. I often look around

and wonder who is in the room. I imagine an unsaved construction worker attending church for the first time and enduring awful lyrics and cringy mini-sermons from the worship leader.

A first-time visitor just became a last-time visitor.

Don't say or sing things that make people uncomfortable. We don't need any more sloppy, wet kisses from Heaven. Please make it stop.

I'm not talking about the Holy Spirit's conviction when I say we shouldn't make people uncomfortable. Conviction is always uncomfortable, and it should be. When the Lord prompts you to change course, you feel it.

I'm referring to the unnecessary absurdities that creep into some praise and worship sets. We want to take time to encourage those in the service, but we need to be far more intentional with what we say. I'll deal with that in the next chapter.

Another worship leader wanted the congregation to lift their hands and shout, "Fill me, Daddy," for the next sixty seconds.

Time for a bathroom break.

It's not good when you glance around the sanctuary and see most people looking sheepishly at their shoes. You don't want to do or say things that snap people out of their worship connection.

Also, can we stop saying "daddy" when referring to God? That's not what *Abba* means. In the first century, it simply meant "father" or "my father."

As Greek scholar, Murray Harris wrote in his book *Navigating Tough Texts*:

> For Christians, young or old, to address God as "Daddy" is totally inappropriate, for in English usage the term is too casual and flippant and unassuming to be used in addressing the Lord God Almighty, the Creator and Sustainer of all things.[1]

When I was younger, I would wince when I heard others my age refer to their father as "my old man." I couldn't imagine saying such a thing about my father.

There's a balance between understanding that we have a close, personal relationship with our heavenly Father and remembering we're addressing the almighty God of the universe.

SEEING THROUGH A DIFFERENT LENS

There's a fine line between not saying awkward things because you know unsaved people are in the room and compromising the truth because of those people.

The examples I've already given you aren't just embarrassing to hear for unbelievers; they're uncomfortable for believers, too.

However, you cross a line when you refuse to talk about things that are genuinely scriptural because you think they will make unbelievers uncomfortable.

A few years ago, I was listening to a church growth video. The speaker encouraged people who would talk to the congregation to rethink their religious jargon, knowing that they wanted to communicate more clearly to unchurched people.

"We've got to be careful," he said. "You may have been in church for a long time, but don't say things like, 'How many of you are glad you're washed in the blood?' He continued with his reasoning. "The visitor might think, 'Oh, no. Do they wash people in blood in this church?'"

The problem is that if you follow this advice, you'd be embarrassed to mention things found in Scripture that are central doctrinal truths for the church!

I'm not teaching "seeker sensitivity" in this chapter. I have a major problem with the modern thought that we should arrange our church services in such a way that an unbeliever would never feel uncomfortable at any point. By all means, operate with excellence, but never compromise the truth to make people comfortable in their sin.

If you want to be more mindful of those who may not know the Bible yet, there are different ways to say the same thing and get the same result.

You could just as easily ask, "How many of you are glad that your sins are forgiven because of the blood of Jesus?" This asks the same question more clearly while not compromising God's Word.

RETHINK YOUR RESPONSIBILITY

I once asked a minister how to communicate controversial biblical truths more effectively. When you speak about certain subjects, you can feel resistance from the crowd.

However, just because these topics are controversial and people may not understand them doesn't mean they don't need to be taught.

If you've ever given medication to a pet, you know that sometimes the best way to do it is to crush it up and put it in their food. They may not eat it by itself, but by putting it in their food, you're presenting it to them in a way they can ingest it.

The same principle is true here. The minister told me something that I'll never forget. He said, "It's not just our responsibility to tell people the truth. It's our responsibility to tell them the truth in a way they can receive it."

That's such a powerful revelation. As I pointed out, you can say things two different ways and have different results.

Be careful not to be a condescending worship leader. It's an instant turn-off. I'm disappointed to hear worship leaders say things like, "Oh, come on! You didn't come ready to praise the Lord today. Lift your hands!"

Or sometimes you'll hear something like, "I thought this was a Pentecostal church! Does anybody in here have the Holy Ghost?"

These are unnecessary antagonistic phrases. It's better not to use them. Why would you want to turn the congregation against you as you're leading them in worship?

Also, please don't use youth group banter with the crowd. It's terrible, and you've heard it before.

"How many are excited to be in the house of the Lord today?"

No cheering

"Come on, you can do better than that. Who's excited?"

Still no cheering

"Aww, let me try this side. Is anyone excited?"

It's not children's church.

Instead, encourage the congregation by faith. Say things that build their anticipation and prepare them to receive. For example, "Let's lift our hands to the Lord. He's here right now to touch every one of us as we worship him by faith."

We can still encourage the congregation to interact, but it should be accompanied by a statement of truth meant to provoke their faith.

As the worship leader, you set the stage for people to receive from God. Their hearts should be in proper position by the time the sermon starts.

When preaching, Billy Graham used to say he remembered that in every pew, there was a broken heart. That's a wonderful reminder. Use that same mindset as you lead worship, and remember that, most likely, there are unbelievers in the room.

NOTES

1. Harris, Murray J. Navigating Tough Texts: A Guide to Problem Passages in the New Testament. Lexham Press, 2020.

Checklist

(1) Each week, ask God to prepare you to minister to the believers *and* the unbelievers in the room.

(2) Ensure that analogies from your personal stories don't diminish God's authority or make him seem foolish or childish. Remember his holiness and power.

(3) Can you clarify your exhortations and make them more understandable for those unfamiliar with the Bible?

(4) In retrospect, can you identify times when you've been condescending or antagonistic? How can you deliver the same message differently?

(5) Set a goal to be able to communicate things that are equally dynamic to believers and unbelievers alike.

IF YOUR SPIRIT IS VOID OF REVELATION, YOUR WORDS WILL BE EMPTY & POWERLESS.

COMMANDMENT SIX
HAVE SOMETHING TO SAY

"How many know his love is reckless, amen? How many know today that he's chasing us down? He fights until we're found. He leaves the ninety-nine. Let's sing it together."

Ah, the worship leader whose exhortation is simply the beginning lyrics from his upcoming song. We've all heard it.

I'm not rejecting this practice as a whole. There are ways you can do it without seeming corny or forced. However, I want to suggest a better avenue for you as a worship leader.

Nothing will ever be more powerful than the revelation you've received during your devotional time with the Lord.

Have you ever considered that David's Psalms were simply the overflow of his time in God's presence?

His descriptions are so accurate and detailed. You can tell he's not describing what he thinks. It's not philosophy. He's describing what he has experienced. Look how he refers to himself:

> I sought the Lord, and he answered me and delivered me from all my fears. Those who look to him are radiant, and their faces shall never be ashamed. This poor man cried, and the Lord heard him and saved him out of all his troubles.
>
> Psalm 34:4-6 ESV

He wrote, "*This* poor man cried." David's relationship with the Lord is well documented in Scripture. God called David a man after his own heart (Acts 13:22). David had a close connection with God.

As I've said before, it was such a tight connection that David chose to fight Goliath when he heard the Philistine mocking God. The Lord didn't have to tell David to fight Goliath; David's love was enough to provoke him to battle.

A close connection with the Holy Spirit produces

extraordinary insight. Having something powerful to share with the congregation originates from your prayer life, your time in God's Word, and the voices you allow to teach and impart to you.

As I wrote in the chapter about prayer, you can tell when someone doesn't pray consistently. The emptiness is evident. We should never be that way.

You must always fill yourself up in God's presence before you pour yourself out to others. You cannot give what you don't have.

When Jesus spoke about private dedication, he promised to openly reward anyone who would humbly seek God's face.

> But when you pray, go into your room and shut the door and pray to your Father who is in secret. And your Father who sees in secret will reward you.
>
> Matthew 6:6 ESV

One reward from the Lord is the supernatural power released through prayer (James 5:16). There's a clear difference between a worship leader who prays and one who doesn't.

There's a very tangible anointing when a person of prayer is leading. They're taking you somewhere that's very familiar to them. They know God's presence. Nothing can ever take the place of the anointing. Skill, personality, charisma, and performance ability are all great, but without the anointing, they're worthless.

Remember that we're not trying to entertain; our goal is to successfully lead others into God's presence and to a place where they can properly receive His Word. If we do those two things, we've succeeded.

The following five parameters will allow you to create more dynamic exhortations during your worship services.

1. BE SCRIPTURAL

The first thing you must remember is that God will not honor anything contrary to his Word. Truly, he is watching over his Word to perform it. (See Jeremiah 1:12.)

When you exhort the congregation during worship, it should be based on Scripture. This will often stem from your private time in God's Word.

Nothing is worse than a leader trying to make a point from a life experience without a scriptural basis. Sometimes, those listening struggle to understand what's being said. Be clear. Be biblical. The strongest level of anointing you'll have on your exhortation is when you're driving home a scriptural principle. Specifically when describing God's greatness or Christ's majestic nature.

Come into each service with something from the Bible that you can use to encourage the congregation.

2. BE ENCOURAGING

Never, I repeat, never focus on what's negative. Focus on God's greatness. That's what praise is. Faith is putting complete trust in the one you serve. No matter what you're facing, his supernatural power is more than able to deliver you.

The people you're speaking to have already heard every bad report floating around. Most people don't come from an atmosphere of faith, so they don't need us to tell them how bad things are in the world.

They need us to paint a picture on the canvas of their minds that shows what their breakthrough is going to look like. The writers do this throughout the Psalms.

Though some Psalms are meant to be encouragements and others are cries for help, some describe the future of those who put their trust in the Lord. This future is always a victorious one full of blessings.

> Praise the Lord! Blessed is the man who fears the Lord, who greatly delights in his commandments! His offspring will be mighty in the land; the generation of the upright will be blessed. Wealth and riches are in his house, and his righteousness endures forever.
>
> Psalm 112:1-3 ESV

As you can see, the Psalmist (most likely David) is talking about the future blessings that will come to someone who fears the Lord.

You should incorporate these same types of encouragements into your worship services. They should always be filled with faith and point toward victory.

3. BE JOYFUL

There's a reason I spent an entire chapter discussing the importance of joy. It's contagious, breeds strength, and is God's fuel for your purpose.

I can't think of anything less engaging than a worship leader devoid of joy. It sucks the life out of an entire service. Trust me. I've had to take the microphone afterward and try my best to resurrect the living dead.

That's the opposite of what a praise and worship

service is supposed to do. Obviously, your joy has to be genuine. People can spot a facade from miles away. Not everyone who acts happy is happy.

> Laughter can conceal a heavy heart, but when the laughter ends, the grief remains.
> Proverbs 14:13 NLT

I'm not talking about "cheerleader face." We're not building hype for the sake of excitement. As leaders, we must carry true joy that we can impart to others.

As I wrote in the first chapter, to rejoice is to *show* great joy or delight. God commanded us to not just have joy but to show it, as well.

Above all, God's command should prove that joy is not optional but a choice. If joy is the result of provoking God's presence (Psalm 16:11), we should already be filled with joy *before* we lead others into it.

Can you imagine how ridiculous it would be if someone hired a golf instructor who had to learn the game alongside the pupil who hired him?

You should already have the element you're leading others into. Again, you can only give what you already have.

4. BE INTERACTIVE

As a leader, you should be assertive. It's okay to give instruction as you worship. The Bible provides us with a precedent for that kind of interaction. The Psalmists often command God's people to interact with praise and worship.

"Magnify the Lord with me. Let us exalt his name together," one Psalm reads. Another commands us to "Clap your hands all you people and shout unto God with a voice of triumph."

Psalm 107 declares, "Oh give thanks unto the Lord for he is good." These are commands to the reader to join the Psalmist in praising God.

We should do the same. Encourage people to clap or lift their hands, shout unto God, raise their voices, and sing or join you in thanking God for his goodness. Don't use seeker-sensitive phrases like, "If you feel comfortable, lift your hands." Whether or not we're comfortable is irrelevant. We praise the way we do because the Bible commands it.

Your carnal nature will never want to praise God. You have to force your flesh to do what the Bible says. Paul wrote that he had to subdue his flesh every day. (See 1 Corinthians 9:27.)

5. BE BRIEF

Finally, you don't have to go on forever. After all, you're not preaching the message; you're leading worship. As my grandfather used to say, "You don't have to be eternal to be divine."

Some exhortations may be longer than others, but as a rule, encourage the congregation as much as you can while still focusing on the praise and worship.

Long, drawn-out talking between songs breaks the flow of the service. It's not about us; it's about the Lord. Do your best to break a spirit of heaviness, build joy, produce faith, and lead others into God's presence.

Let these parameters act as loose guidelines to help you. Focus on the end goal. It's not about singing songs; it's about taking others to a place where their spirits can easily receive God's Word and become fruitful.

(1) Have you fallen into the trap of using the words of the next song as a lazy exhortation in transition?

(2) Have you taken the time to prepare your encouragements or exhortations in between songs? If not, why haven't you?

(3) As you take time to prepare your worship set, ask God to give you insight into Scripture that will encourage the congregation in their worship.

(4) Have you found yourself carrying heaviness or frustration onto the platform before worship? Did you notice it affecting what you said to the congregation?

(5) Have you been embarrassed to engage the congregation interactively in the past? Can you identify what holds you back?

COMMANDMENT SEVEN
NO UNSCRIPTURAL SONGS

When I began my evangelistic ministry and started booking revivals, churches would call and ask if there were any worship songs I'd like them to sing. I would always tell them to sing whatever they felt, and I'd flow with it.

I don't do that anymore.

Not that there are specific songs that I want churches to sing, but there may be songs I *don't want* them to sing.

Just because a song plays on a popular Christian radio station doesn't mean you should incorporate it into your worship service.

Some songs are simply unscriptural. Songs that don't line up with God's Word are a problem because they contradict what God said. When you disagree with God, that's evil because, essentially, you're calling God a liar.

THAT'S NOT WHAT GOD SAID

When the twelve spies entered Canaan to observe the Promised Land, they encountered the giants and saw their fortified cities.

Ten of the twelve delivered a fearful report to the assembly when they returned to describe what they had seen. The Bible describes their conclusion in a very negative light:

> So they brought the Israelites an evil report of the land which they had scouted out, saying, The land through which we went to spy it out is a land that devours its inhabitants. And all the people that we saw in it are men of great stature.
> Numbers 13:32 AMPC

Notice that the Bible calls it an *evil report*. Modern translations may use the words "bad" or "discouraging" to describe their summary.

However, I want to focus on the term "evil report"

because of what's truly happening in this passage. The Hebrew word here can be translated as slander, defamation, or an evil report, as in Numbers 13:32.

To slander or defame is to make a false statement that will damage someone's reputation. That's why describing the ten spies' report of the Promised Land as "evil" is accurate.

God told them he had given them the land. He told them to take it. They contradicted God by saying that they were unable to take the land.

God said they were able; they said they were unable. Who was lying? Hint: not God.

When we say or sing things that contradict God's written Word, it's evil. I refuse to call God a liar, and neither should you.

I RIPPED UP MY SERMON

It never seemed to fail. I would announce that I was going to be preaching on healing and praying for the sick, and a worship leader would sing a song that would wreck the atmosphere of faith.

I was holding a revival in the Northeast, and it happened again. Just before I took the microphone, the worship leader launched into the bridge of *Blessed Be the Name of the Lord*. The bridge is a quotation from the

Book of Job, which says, "He gives and takes away."

The problem is that after Job said these things, he was rebuked by his friend, and then God rebuked him. By the end of the book, Job had to admit,

> You asked, 'Who is this that questions my wisdom with such ignorance?' It is I—and I was talking about things I knew nothing about, things far too wonderful for me.
>
> Job 42:3 NLT

Job was attributing his trouble to the Lord. Why would we want to sing songs repeating the confession of a man God rebuked for saying what he did?

After the worship leader began singing that song, I sat down on the front row, ditched my sermon, and began to write a new one called "He Gives and Takes Away."

When people sing or talk about that passage, they mean, "Sometimes God gives good things, and sometimes he takes them away."

I hate it when people blame God for their trouble. God didn't take your loved one to Heaven before their time. God isn't evil.

I started listing all the things God gives: salvation, healing, deliverance, blessing, peace, and joy. Afterward, I listed all the things he takes away: sin, sickness, poverty, brokenness, anxiety, and depression. When I got the microphone, I preached it with all the fire I had inside. I refuse to slander God.

GOD DOESN'T ANOINT EVERYTHING

If we're singing things that constantly misrepresent God's character and nature, why would he approve of it? He doesn't. Just as we don't pray in a way that contradicts God's Word, we also don't worship that way.

God is always watching over his Word to perform it (Jeremiah 1:12). Arguably, one of the most critical passages in the Bible is in Numbers chapter 23:

> God is not man, that he should lie, or a son of man, that he should change his mind. Has he said, and will he not do it? Or has he spoken, and will he not fulfill it?
>
> Numbers 23:19 ESV

One minister said, "God doesn't hate lies because he loves the truth. He hates lies because he is the truth." (See John 14:6.) I refuse to say or sing things that go against what's written.

I've heard worship leaders drone on about how unworthy we are to receive God's blessings and stand before him.

The truth is God *made us* worthy to receive. Because we believe in Jesus' name, he gave us the power to become his sons (John 1:12). If we weren't worthy, why would he bless us with *every* spiritual blessing? (See Ephesians 1:3.)

When worship leaders say things like that, it shows that either they don't know the Bible or they don't understand they're contradicting what God said and what he has done for us.

This is a rookie mistake you cannot afford to make. Don't ever say things because you've heard others say them. Say what the Bible says.

This goes back to the previous commandment of "Have Something to Say." As a worship leader, you must be well-versed in God's Word. Bible knowledge isn't just a discipline for Pastors.

As you dedicate yourself to being scripturally accurate, you'll notice the power of God's presence increase in manifestation in your worship.

God's Spirit always operates in agreement with his Word. God will never do something that he didn't first say. This is such a fundamental principle that God always reveals his Word *first*.

> For the Lord GOD does nothing without revealing his secret to his servants the prophets.
>
> Amos 3:7 ESV

What you say and sing is essential. We can't be flippant when it comes to our confession.

WORDS MATTER

Over the years, there have been popular worship songs that don't make sense. A notable example is the song "Reckless Love." Though it's a beautiful song, the concept doesn't make biblical sense.

To describe God's love for humanity as reckless is foolish at best. "Reckless" means "To act without thinking or caring about the consequences."

To think this is what God did by sending Christ or giving us the gospel shows a gross lack of biblical knowledge.

Even a cursory reading of John 3:16 proves this thought process false. God didn't send Jesus recklessly; he sent him so that "Whoever believes in him should not perish but have eternal life."

God's kingdom functions on the principle of sowing and reaping. Paul reminded the Galatians that

God's system would not be mocked. Whatever a man or woman sows is what they will reap. (See Galatians 6:7.) God created the system. He *never* does anything randomly. He always acts with purpose.

As a logical thinker, I could never bring myself to utter those lyrics if I were ever in a church that sang that song.

WRONG WORDS = WRONG PERSPECTIVE

We should never focus on who we used to be before being born again. Many Christians retain their guilt and shame after conversion, and the devil uses it to keep them from receiving from God.

I like the phrase, "I am who God says I am." I'm not what I feel like, what the world says about me, or who I used to be. I'm who God says I am in his Word.

Take care not to sing songs that confuse your identity in Christ. That mindset is destructive and will limit your ability to accomplish your purpose.

Most hymns, which have been part of the church for hundreds of years, reinforce theological truths. Our singing, not just our preaching, should reflect the biblical truths we believe.

In 2011, Casting Crowns released a song called *Jesus, Friend of Sinners*. Though their intentions may have been good, the lyrics aren't helpful.

The first pre-chorus of the song says, "I'm so double-minded. A plank-eyed saint with dirty hands and a heart divided." I don't know how you feel, but I could never sing those words. I'd never make that confession about myself.

By saying that you're double-minded, you're saying that you're unstable and not able to receive anything from God! (See James 1:6-8.)

What Christian in their right mind would sing that they have a divided heart? Again, just because a song has become popular doesn't mean we should sing it.

I encourage you to examine the songs that you plan to sing. Are they scriptural? Do they contradict God's Word? If so, leave them behind. God honors his Word. When we sing what his Word says, we can watch him perform it.

(1) Have any songs struck you as unscriptural? Can you list the biblical reasons why?

(2) Are there any songs you're singing that contradict Scripture? Can a word or words be easily changed to align the song with the Bible?

(3) Have you ever felt convicted about singing a particular song?

(4) Who was the first to alter God's Word, making it say what God never said?

(5) Do you currently have a screening process for how you choose worship songs?

COMMANDMENT EIGHT
MASTER TRANSITIONS

The worship leader is singing the final chorus, and the song is finishing its climax and coming to an end. Every hand in the room is lifted high, and the worship is at a crescendo.

The song abruptly ends, and the sanctuary grows quiet. The singers are now standing awkwardly on the stage while the musicians are moving their papers around, setting the chord charts in place for the next song on the set list.

There's some coughing in the sanctuary as the guitar player retunes one of his strings. The wonderful worship moment that enraptured every heart moments ago has been wiped away by a common mistake — *a poor transition.*

I probably don't have to ask you if you've experienced something like this because unless you attend a megachurch or one of the select few churches that operate with a high level of excellence in the media department, you definitely have.

However, this is a mistake that can be (and should be) easily avoided. Leading others in worship is much different than a concert. We're not performing for the enjoyment of the audience; we're guiding them into a place of personal and corporate worship.

The point is that our focus should be on the Lord. Anything that breaks our focus or takes us out of that moment of worship and praise is an obstacle that must be eliminated.

NEVER AGAIN!

I was in a service one Sunday morning at a church that had just launched. Because they were new, they didn't have a worship team yet.

To fill the gap, they were using YouTube videos to worship with the congregation. After one worship video ended, the next began . . . but not without an ad playing first.

"BOGO holiday sales are on!" It blared through the sound system. As you know, commercials are usually louder than the content they follow. It was startling and very embarrassing for the pastor and the congregation. Fortunately, it was an ad that could be skipped after five seconds.

Later that afternoon, I was at lunch with the pastor and his wife, and they began to apologize profusely for the issue that happened.

"I don't mind," I said. "Mistakes happen. The question I have for you is, what plan do you have in place so that it never happens again?"

They stared at me blankly as though they didn't know what I meant. Then, they began to make excuses about how they're not very tech-savvy, and they'd try to address it.

Obviously, there are a number of things they could have done to ensure it didn't happen again: buy a premium YouTube subscription, create their own playlists from a paid streaming service, or play the songs from a CD or hard drive.

Again, mistakes will happen, but because we desire excellence, we should try to think through every possible scenario *ahead of time* and take steps to prevent simple mistakes from occurring.

It's not just about the state of our hearts. We want to please the Lord with our excellence as we pursue him. Even in the Old Testament, God commanded excellence in worship. God's people didn't halfheartedly praise or worship him.

> Sing a new song of praise to him; play skillfully on the harp, and sing with joy.
> Psalm 33:3 NLT

King David, the man after God's own heart, took his praise and worship seriously. Even when he could have easily commanded others to praise on his behalf, he got in front of the crowd and danced with all his might. He gave it his all. (See 2 Samuel 6:14.)

Because we're leading others, we should work to ensure that every potential distraction is identified and removed.

OVERCOMING TRANSITION KILLERS

Transitions are where most worship teams suffer. In fact, it's where most worship services suffer. I want to encourage you to identify and work to eliminate these very common problems that occur during transitions.

1. Awkward silences between songs

As I previously mentioned, one of the mistakes that can ruin a worship service is not knowing what to do between the different songs in your set. Silence while everyone prepares themselves for the next song is a mistake that you should avoid.

What can you do instead? There are several options. First, have the keyboard player or guitar player continue to play worshipfully between songs. Ideally, you can place two songs of the same key next to each other in your set list.

Secondly, the worship leader or a singer who will lead the next song can step forward and encourage or exhort the congregation before the next song begins.

Finally, you can finish a song with a crescendo by having the congregation clap their hands, rejoice, or shout to the Lord. Obviously, you don't want to end every song the same way, as it will become monotonous, predictable, and lose its impact.

2. Abrupt breaks and harsh changes

Nothing feels less prepared than a song coming to an end followed by a harsh key change. Obviously, if you can't place songs of the same key next to each other in your set list, there will have to be a key change.

One solution is to come up with a chord pattern that transitions between two different keys seamlessly. This can almost become a game for the musicians.

Years ago, as a music director, I would challenge

myself to create chord patterns that would transition from one key to a totally unrelated key without sounding harsh or out of place.

For example, the keys of E flat and A are not interrelated because those two notes are tritones, and when played in succession, they sound very dissonant and "wrong" to the normal ear.

My goal would be to create a pattern that connected those two keys and still sounded smooth. That way, everything would sound fluid, and no one would be pulled away from being in God's presence because of a needless distraction.

A modern solution is to use ambient pads that play behind your worship team. The root note of the key you're in plays throughout the song. When the song finishes, the pad will transition and fade to the next key of the upcoming song.

Even if no one is playing during this transition, it keeps something going in the background and creates a smooth texture as the new song begins. You can use software like Playback, which is produced by Multitracks.com or Ableton Live.

3. Beginning the service

Excellence should carry over to our schedules as well. If we tell people our services begin at 10:00 am, we shouldn't begin at 10:07 am. I've tuned in to church livestreams and watched as musicians amble up to the platform and slowly plug in their instruments while talking and laughing—terrible transition!

There's no sense of urgency or excellence. Let's not waste people's time. It's just as disrespectful to be flippant with the worship schedule as it is to show up to your job late or be tardy for a business lunch with your boss.

As you begin the service, combine some of the other commandments we've already covered. Be joyful and have something encouraging and faith-filled to say. Know the direction you're headed, and move forward confidently.

4. Know what's happening in the service

Are there video announcements before or after your worship set? Is someone coming to address the crowd at any point during your worship set? Who is taking the microphone after you're finished, and what will they be doing?

These are all important questions that need to be answered before you begin the service. Imagine starting a song just as the media team lowers the lights and starts a video because you didn't know it was happening. *Awkward.*

What if a pastor or leader approaches the platform to speak to the congregation, but you've moved on to the next song, and the intro is already playing? *Awkward.*

Does your leadership know what your last song will be? Do they know when to come and make the transition?

Far too often, I've watched worship leaders try to catch the eyes of the pastor to let them know they just finished the last song of the set while the pastor is either standing with his eyes closed or browsing his notes on the front row.

Of course, we want to be led by the Spirit. It's one of the commandments we cover in this book. However, there's a big difference between being led by the Spirit and being unprepared. Never mistake one for the other.

Many churches use software like Planning Center Services to keep everything in check and make sure everyone knows what's happening ahead of time.

5. Be aware of possible technical issues

We all know that some technical issues are simply out of our hands. I've always joked that when no one is looking, there are "platform gnomes" who come and mess with audio levels, EQs, and cable connections.

But many times, proper rehearsals and sound checks will solve most of the issues. If there's a new piece of gear or software that hasn't yet been tested, it's not the best idea to audition it during the Sunday morning service.

Unplugged cables, not knowing which microphone is yours, improper monitor levels, excessive feedback, poor EQ, or hums from equipment that's not properly grounded are the result of poor preparation or a sign of technical ignorance.

The good news is that these problems can be easily fixed. What's not easy to fix is complacency. If someone has no desire to excel in their craft, it's hard to motivate that person.

Resolve as many technical issues as possible through proper rehearsals and sound checks. If you lack specific knowledge, find YouTube tutorials or pay someone to train you in that area.

6. Be attentive to the minister

In most churches, the worship team will come back to the platform at the end of the service as the minister transitions into altar ministry.

It's frustrating when the worship team takes too long to come back. I've been in services where the worship team wasn't even in the sanctuary when the minister called for them. Remember that this is not a "gig," and you're not a rock star. We're servants of the most high God. Be watchful and sensitive to what the Holy Spirit is doing in the service.

Is there a song that the Lord may be leading you to sing or play during altar ministry? Which way does the minister seem to be going? Will he give a call for salvation? Is he going to pray for healing? Is this a prayer service? Do you have songs ready for those situations?

Always be tuned in and ready to go when it's time to step up and minister through the gift God has given you.

I WAS ALMOST THROWN OUT OF CHURCH

I was very young when I went to Bible school. At eighteen, I left home and moved out west. When I arrived at college, I auditioned and quickly became the church organist.

One Sunday morning, as our pastor was preaching in the beautiful, 5,000 seat sanctuary, I felt the Spirit begin to move. There was a victorious spirit of faith on the message. I did what I had always done in those situations — I ran up on the platform and jumped on the Hammond organ.

This was common to me. If the preacher really started preaching, the organist would play behind him. Apparently, that wasn't how it worked at this church.

The members of the pastoral staff were scowling at me from across the platform. I was starting to feel like I had made the wrong move.

I stayed with it and kept playing. When the service ended, the pastor came over to the organ.

"I haven't heard organ playing like that in a long time!" He said. He had enjoyed it, and I had made the right move by being attentive and following the leading of the Holy Spirit.

Being led by the Spirit is an indispensable skill that every worship leader must hone, and we'll cover that in-depth throughout the next chapter.

(1) Do you spend any time planning the transitions of your worship set? If not, make time to think about that when you plan your set lists.

(2) If you've had transition problems, what is the biggest factor that contributes to them?

(3) What steps do you currently take to ensure that you'll limit any technical problems that could arise?

(4) If you follow a planned service order, consider writing the transitions on the list so that everyone knows what to expect.

(5) How a service begins and ends is important. Spend time preparing how you'll start and finish the service unless the Spirit flows in a different way.

COMMANDMENT NINE
FOLLOW THE LEADER

My band members laughed as I showed them the setlist of songs we'd be playing that night. A new bass player, whom we'd never met before, was joining us for that service.

He glanced around at the other members, wondering why they were laughing. Seeing his expression, one of them quickly explained.

"We might do *one* of these songs. Just hang on and flow wherever we go," my guitar player said. I knew that comment was coming.

He said it because my band knows I rarely follow the setlist. Furthermore, I don't provide a setlist for the band or singers in many of my worship services. I'll tell them the first song, then begin.

For some, that would cause a heart attack. No Planning Center? No chord charts? No multitracks? No transitional drone pads? (It's okay if you're unfamiliar with these terms. Keep reading.)

I'm not against planning or preparation. You *should* prepare. I'm not trying to discourage you from being efficient and organized, but I want to make an important point in this chapter: nothing is more important than being led by God's Spirit.

Some may argue that God can lead you ahead of time and show you how to proceed. That's true.

However, in my experience, he leads me while I'm in the middle of worshiping him.

For anyone involved in platform ministry, you understand that it takes faith to make a mid-service change with your team—and maybe that's why God does it that way. Faith pleases him. You have to release your pride and follow the Spirit's leading.

You may ask, "How will it turn out?" Though it's a valid question, it really doesn't matter. I'd rather obey the Holy Spirit and look foolish than give a polished performance in disobedience.

We know that God's ways are higher than our ways, and his thoughts are higher than our thoughts. (See Isaiah 55:8-9.) Follow him no matter the direction.

SONGS IN THE SPIRIT

One of the things that Scripture commands believers to do is worship God with spiritual songs.

> And do not get drunk with wine, for that is debauchery, but be filled with the Spirit, addressing one another in psalms and hymns and spiritual songs, singing and making melody to the Lord with your heart,
>
> Ephesians 5:18-19 ESV

When Paul writes "psalms," it's undoubtedly a reference to the book of Psalms. These can be recited as a form of worship. Hymns are songs that have already been written. What are spiritual songs?

We can break this concept into three distinct categories. First, in his notes on Ephesians 5:19, Finis Dake suggests this could be a reference to singing in the Spirit or unknown tongues, as Paul described in 1 Corinthians 14:15-16.

Secondly, this could represent the Holy Spirit giving you a spontaneous song at that very moment. I've had this happen to me many times. Not long ago, I was at my father's spring campmeeting. The morning

I was scheduled to speak, I woke up with a chorus in my spirit. It was so fully developed that I thought it was an old song I'd heard before. I continued to sing it, wondering where I'd heard it until I realized I never had!

The Lord was giving me a new song for that morning's service. The song, *Spirit of Faith*, which we later released on all streaming platforms, supplemented what I was preaching that morning.

I never sat down to write a new song. It was already in me when I woke up. It was from the Spirit. That's a version of a spiritual song. God has often given me brand-new songs while I was in the middle of a worship service.

Finally, I believe a spiritual song can be the Lord leading you to sing an already-established song at a certain point in the service. Maybe you planned to sing something else, but the Lord leads you to sing something different that's not even on the list.

It takes faith to deviate from your plans, but following the Lord's leading is always worth it.

Once, I was leading worship for my father in Toledo, Ohio. As he began to minister to people at the end of the service, my sister, Megan, and I began to lead a song that we hadn't planned to sing: *Alpha and Omega*.

We sang that song without changing to something

else for over an hour as God instantly healed people. I don't think many people realize how vital music is to the moving of God's Spirit.

The prophet Elisha called for a harpist to play for him. When the harpist played, the hand of God came upon Elisha, and he began to prophesy (2 Kings 3:15).

When David played his harp in King Saul's court, the evil spirit that troubled Saul's mind had to leave him alone (1 Samuel 16:23).

When three enemy armies joined together to destroy God's people, the tribe of Judah advanced against them with only instruments. As they sang and played, God fought their battle for them and gave them total victory (2 Chronicles 20:22-24).

We have to be sensitive to the Holy Spirit as we lead worship. It's not a concert, performance, or a show. It's a supernatural transaction with God. As we praise him, he moves on our behalf.

7 PRACTICAL TIPS FOR FLOWING IN THE SPIRIT

1. Don't be romantic about your list.
Sometimes, we can be so in love with the perfect list we've created for our service that we don't want to mess it up by altering it or deviating from it.

You might say, "Yeah, but song A transitions so seamlessly into song B!" Or maybe there's a new song on the list with a bridge you love, and you don't want to remove it from the service.

It might sound odd, but your setlist can become an idol if you allow it to guide and control you rather than following the Holy Spirit. Preparation is fine, but never let your plans cancel God's plans.

Realize that the service belongs to the Lord. Let him make the changes he wants to make. If he leads you, follow his direction without delay.

2. Be prayerful and focus on the Lord.

One way to be ready to flow at any moment is to stay sensitive to the Holy Spirit. Avoid distractions before the service begins, particularly getting caught up in long, drawn-out conversations before you worship.

Guard yourself from carnality and foolishness. You don't have to become a robot, but focus on your task. It's vital.

We're not just singing a few songs; we're ministering and leading others into God's presence. We're preparing people to receive the Word.

If we allow distractions or carnality and ignore our sensitivity to the Spirit, we'll miss important prompts that the Lord can give us in the moment.

The last thing I want is to lead a fleshly performance. I want to worship in spirit and truth until people are prepared to hear from God and receive what he has for them.

3. Teach your team to be flexible.
One thing that can hinder you from being able to flow is the rigid nature of preparation and planning. As I said previously, we should plan and prepare but never allow ourselves to depend on the plans or the tools we use in preparation.

For example, many worship teams (including worship leaders) can only complete a worship service if their chord charts are in front of them. They depend on those charts to worship the Lord, and flowing is impossible.

Internalize your songs as much as you can. No matter what song comes next, you'll be able to follow along. It's essential to develop your ear training. Rather than depending on a chart, you can hear the chord changes and follow along.

Even if you're not yet at that stage or skill level, you can still memorize worship songs as you learn them. Flexibility is a significant factor in being able to flow in the Spirit.

Sometimes, teams that use multitracks to supplement their band may hesitate to worship with an unplanned song because they don't have accompanying tracks. They may worry that the music will sound "empty" and less professional.

Again, I would much rather follow the leading of the Holy Spirit. The anointing will bless people as it flows and will significantly impact the service. At that point, the perceived difference in the sound of the worship will become irrelevant. Don't be afraid to be flexible.

4. Don't worry about mistakes.

Being a perfectionist is a two-edged sword. On one hand, we always want to do our very best for the Lord. We don't want to offer God a sloppy attempt rather than a life of excellence.

But sometimes, we're so preoccupied with perfectionism that we won't step out by faith to do what the Lord asks us to do. We won't lead a particular song because everyone may not know it or we haven't practiced it enough.

In these situations, perfectionism becomes an idol that keeps us from being led by God's Spirit. As I wrote earlier, I'd rather obey the Holy Spirit and look foolish than give a polished performance in disobedience. Don't let perfectionism stop you.

5. Don't worry about what people think.

When I started as a worship leader, I'd get so embarrassed if I played a wrong chord or missed the song's timing for a few measures. Then, I found out that almost no one notices those things. Most people aren't musicians and can't tell if you played the right or wrong chord.

There were times when I walked off the platform feeling discouraged because of my musical mistakes, only to be met by someone who said, "That's one of the best worship services we've had."

Though I was preoccupied with my blunders, God was still able to minister to them during the worship service.

What a surprise.

The fear of what people will think if you try something new or different from what you planned is a major obstacle that you must ignore.

We don't lead worship to please people; we do it to *prepare* people and please God.

6. Be aware of what's happening in the service.

Few things are more frustrating than a musician or worship leader who is oblivious to what's happening in the service. I don't just mean they're on their phone or daydreaming. Those things should be a given.

It's dishonorable to be disengaged.

Understanding how to follow what happens during the service is one of the keys to worship leading that will put you a cut above the rest. Any effective worship leader must learn to flow with the minister who is speaking. Here are a few questions you can ask to prepare for the end of the service:

- What is the main idea of the sermon?

- How does it seem like the minister will end the service? (e.g., With an altar call for salvation, praying for the sick, taking communion, praise and worship, etc.)

- What song(s) can I have ready if he ends the service this way?

- Did he mention any specific songs during his sermon?

By paying attention and asking these questions, you'll remain engaged during the service and be ready to flow as soon as he calls on you.

It's very awkward to be in the middle of an altar call for salvation—a moment of consecration—and the band launches into an upbeat praise song that's headed in a different direction.

Though that may be an extreme example, I've been in many services when something similar happened. Don't be that person.

7. Don't be afraid to kill it if it's not working.
Once, during a revival in Pennsylvania, I felt led to sing a specific song before I preached. I sat down at the piano, picked a key, and played the intro.

The problem was that I hadn't played or sung this song in a long time. When the intro finished, I began singing the first verse and quickly realized the key was too high for my voice.

Rather than screech-howling my way through the song for the next three minutes, I immediately stopped playing the piano.

"Folks," I said, "I'd really like to end the service without a hernia. So, I'm going to find a key that works for my voice." They laughed, and I changed the key. It doesn't have to be awkward. Humor is your best friend.

Sometimes, stepping out to do a song you didn't plan can go awry. If there's a technical issue, don't be afraid to reset.

Other times, I've been in the middle of a song and

felt to switch to another chorus that would work as a medley. When I did, I could feel that it wasn't as strong as the song I had previously sung.

I didn't struggle to push my way through the new song to validate my choice. I sang it through once and switched back to what was working.

In the same way I told you not to be romantic about your song list, don't fall in love with the choices you make in a service. If you feel like the direction you went isn't working, realize that we all make mistakes at times, and go back to what was working.

Don't be discouraged. It's far better to step out by faith and realize that you made a mistake than to never step out at all.

There are times when the Holy Spirit leads us and times when we make decisions. Learn to distinguish between the two. Don't be afraid to step out and flow during a service. Stay flexible.

I cannot overstate the benefits of being led by God's Spirit. It puts us in a position to receive what he wants to do in each service. I've watched miracles take place during moments of Spirit-led worship.

As you step out by faith, I believe you'll experience the Holy Spirit and his power in a greater way than you ever have before.

(1) Have you ever found yourself resisting the urge to make a change the Spirit is leading you to make because it wasn't planned and practiced ahead of time?

(2) Have you ever felt yourself disengaging during the sermon and then scrambling to find a song to close the service? What changes can you make to follow your Pastor more effectively?

(3) Do you ever find yourself paralyzed by people's opinions?

(4) Are there members of the team who aren't currently able to flow with the Spirit in the moment? What can you do to help train them?

(5) Have you ever been distracted by random conversations or encounters before the service? How can you guard yourself and your focus before you begin?

Your gift is either growing or dying; there's no middle ground.

COMMANDMENT TEN
STEADILY IMPROVE YOUR GIFT

When I first began playing the keyboard, YouTube didn't exist. The internet was very young. Because we all used dial-up connections, accessing the internet took about thirty seconds, and a website could take up to three minutes to load.

We had to learn the old-fashioned way—through books. I was so hungry to learn when I started. I remember buying a chord encyclopedia from a local bookstore and rushing home to learn how to play the weird chords (Diminished, augmented, major ninths, etc.).

If I heard a new worship song, I wanted to learn it in all twelve keys. Even if the hand positions felt odd, I'd sit at my keyboard and practice until I could nail every chord change.

Because my father is an evangelist, I attended services in many different churches across America. I would sit in the front row and listen closely during praise and worship.

If the keyboardist or organist played something juicy during the service, I'd run up on the platform at the end and ask him to teach me the change or riff they had played.

Then, I'd learn it in all twelve keys and search for places to play it within the songs I already knew. I wanted to improve so badly.

Because I couldn't Google a chord chart for a worship song I wanted to learn, I had to develop the ability to play by ear. It would frustrate me when I couldn't figure out a chord change in a song from the latest gospel album.

Though God gave me a gift, I had a responsibility to continue developing it. God is pleased when you continually increase the gift or talent he gave you.

The parable of the talents, found in Matthew 25, is the story of a master who gave talents to three of his servants. To the first, he gave five; to the second, he gave two; and to the last, he gave one.

The first two servants invested their talents. When the master returned, they had doubled his money. The final servant buried his talent in the ground. When the master inspected his work, the servant just returned the money to his master.

The master praised and rewarded the first two servants but rebuked the last servant, stripped him of his talent, and cast him into outer darkness. The master referred to the last servant as "wicked."

God expects you to increase whatever he gives you. Here are seven practical ways to continue faithfully increasing your gifts and talents.

1. SCHEDULE YOUR INCREASE

One of the biggest mistakes you can make is to wait until you feel inspired to play or practice your instrument or vocals. Don't wait until you feel like learning something new.

"Pistol" Pete Maravich was one of the greatest ball-handling basketball players of all time. When he was a young man, his father, basketball coach "Press" Maravich, would train him relentlessly making him shoot 100 free throws a day and dribble blindfolded to develop his natural feel.

Pete took his basketball everywhere with him and would constantly practice dribbling. I find it interesting that he didn't only schedule practice time, he also made use of what looked like down time when walking somewhere or watching a movie. Rain or shine, Pistol was practicing and developing his skills.

He didn't wait for a perfect time to practice; he had to make the time. That's the same principle I want you to understand. The ideal time to practice won't just present itself to you. Schedule it.

Put your practice time on your calendar if you have to, and make sure you consistently follow through. Many professional writers write for an hour a day, whether they feel like it or not. Even if they don't use anything they wrote that day, they get words on paper (or screen).

When you schedule practices, you may feel like your progress is slow. Ignore that feeling and put in the time. You're honoring God as you do so.

2. FIND A WAY TO STRETCH YOURSELF

One way to improve your gift is to attempt something that you never thought you could do. When I began playing the keyboard, I purchased a tutorial video produced by jazz legend Chick Corea. Although he was far beyond my talent level, I decided to tackle one of his jazz pieces even though I was a beginner.

I picked Armando's Rhumba. Not only did it have

intricate arpeggio patterns, but it also had differing left and right-hand rhythms. It was beyond my skill level, but I decided to tackle something big and hopefully increase my talent while learning it.

After choosing what song I would learn, I wondered how I was going to start with a project this daunting. Chick Corea must have anticipated that his students would have that thought because his next piece of advice helped me immensely.

3. TAKE SMALL BITES

How do you eat an elephant? One bite at a time. When attempting something big, accomplish it in small chunks. Chick recommended learning a complex piece of music using this method.

He suggested practicing the first bar of the music until I could play it without mistakes. Then, he suggested learning the second bar the same way until I could play them both together smoothly.

Who can't learn one measure of music, right? Using this effective method, I was able to learn not only the Chick Corea piece but many other things after that. I've continued to take small bites as I've progressed through the years.

Don't be discouraged by where you are. Take tiny

steps forward until you realize you've vastly improved from where you started. One way to know you've done this is to use the next tip.

4. LOG YOUR PERFORMANCES

As a child, I'd travel all over the United States with my dad and mom. Sometimes, my sister and I wouldn't see our grandparents for months.

The next time I saw them, they'd often be amazed at how much I'd grown. "Look how big you've gotten," I'd often hear. I didn't feel like there was a drastic change. That's because I'd seen myself every single day. I was observing small growth over time.

My grandparents saw all that growth at once, and it was surprising to them.

We understand the power of "before and after pictures." Whether we're talking about weight loss or a skill you're developing, it isn't easy to realize how far you've come on a day-to-day basis.

By recording yourself and keeping a log of practices and performances, you can compare where you are now to where you were a year ago. You may not even realize how far you've come. This is a very encouraging tip. Keep your growth and improvement in front of your eyes. It will motivate you to keep going.

5. USE FREE TOOLS

Thankfully, we're no longer living in the days of dial-up internet. We have many free resources available to help us improve our gifts. For example, YouTube is your best friend.

We can access endless tutorials, resources, charts, practice drills, mentorship programs, and more online. The explosion of online information is why many children and young teens are at such an advanced skill level with their instruments.

Sometimes, people need help learning how to use a free tool like YouTube to improve their abilities. In my book *Unhang Your Harp*, I wrote: I'm surprised when gifted people are unaware of the top names in their area of gifting. They're oblivious.

If you're a bass player, you should know names like John Patitucci, Victor Wooten, Jaco Pastorius, Stanley Clarke, and Marcus Miller.

For example, as a bass player, I would begin by taking the five names above and finding every YouTube clip of their performances.

Then, I would slowly break down each video and learn to play precisely what they did in that performance. (There are people on YouTube who create many of these tutorials for you.)

You could spend five years just completing that project. Imagine duplicating the bass styles of five of the greatest bass players who ever lived.

Not only would your skill level dramatically increase, but you would also begin to think about playing in the way they thought about it. Your personal style would be developed around the greatest styles of all time.

While learning their licks and grooves, your timing, accuracy, dexterity, and rhythm would become honed like a sharp blade.

That's one way I would use free tools like YouTube to quickly increase my skill level. So many people are dedicated to teaching others and seeing them grow. You can become a part of their communities and join others who are on the same journey as you. There's no longer any excuse not to improve.

6. SURROUND YOURSELF WITH PEOPLE WHO PUSH YOU

Proverbs 27:17 tells us that a friend sharpens a friend in the same way that iron sharpens iron. Refuse to surround yourself with people who dull your blade.

When you play with those who are beyond your skill level, they pull you up to a higher place.

Each member of the band with which I travel and worship plays at a high skill level. When I met each one, I was amazed to watch them play. As we continued traveling together, I learned things from them.

It doesn't matter that they were playing different instruments. I could hear chord changes, riffs, and arpeggios that I could incorporate and emulate.

It's inspiring to hear something new and fresh. One reason we've never played with backing tracks is that we'll change the flow of the song in the middle of playing it.

We'll be in the middle of a praise song, and I'll hear the bass player play a reggae riff. Before you know it, we've all shifted into a reggae arrangement for a few choruses. This wouldn't be possible with an arrangement locked in using tracks.

Playing with those who are at a higher level will stretch you. You'll see and hear things that will change the way you think about the music. There have been times when I have listened to my lead guitar or bass player repeat a riff I've never heard before.

I'll quickly sound it out and play it with them. Then, I'll add to it and morph it into something new.

There are so many benefits to playing with those who are better than you are. Maybe you feel like you don't know anyone like that. It's okay. You can access the best players in history on YouTube using the previous tip. Start there.

7. ASK GOD FOR INCREASE

I can't finish this section of tips without mentioning this one. I've saved it for last because I want it to stick in your mind. Ask God for increase. James wrote:

> If any of you lacks wisdom, let him ask God, who gives generously to all without reproach, and it will be given him.
> James 1:5 ESV

There is absolutely no substitute for divine wisdom. God can anoint your mind to retain knowledge and lead you to do things you couldn't do using your natural wisdom or abilities. Keep in mind that genuine promotion doesn't come from anything or anyone but the Lord. (See Psalm 75:6-7.)

God gave you your gifts and talents and has the power to increase them. Pray and ask him to take you higher.

In the Old Testament, there was a man named Bezalel whom God called to do skillful work that he had never done. Moses wrote:

> The Lord said to Moses, "See, I have called by name Bezalel the son of Uri, son of Hur, of the tribe of Judah, and I have filled him with the Spirit of God, with ability and intelligence, with knowledge and all craftsmanship, to devise artistic designs, to work in gold, silver, and bronze, in cutting stones for setting, and in carving wood, to work in every craft.
>
> Exodus 31:1-5 ESV

Though Bezalel had never done anything the Lord commissioned him to do, God filled him with his Spirit, ability, intelligence, and knowledge. The Lord did this in an Old Testament context. How much more will he do for you because you're his child?

Don't be overwhelmed. Understand that God chose you and anointed you for the task he has given you. The diligent pursuit of excellence is the way to honor God for what he has given you. Don't ever stop moving forward.

I truly believe you will see wonderful testimonies of God's power as you continue to worship him faithfully. In fact, I want to hear what God is doing through your life and ministry. You can always contact me on social media or through our ministry website.

There's one more thing that I want to share with you—*The 11th Commandment*—but I want to give it to you personally. It's the number one weapon that I've seen the devil use against worship leaders and musicians.

I don't want you to fall into this dangerous trap. I want you to "run and not grow weary, and walk and not faint." (See Isaiah 40:31.)

Download it for free by scanning the QR code or browsing to the website listed. May God bless you abundantly as you continue to serve him with your gifts and talents.

Download the 11th Commandment for FREE!

miracleword.com/eleven

(1) Do you notice yourself becoming complacent with your gifts and talents? If so, why?

(2) Do you have someone who pushes you to dive deeper into your gifts and develop your talents?

(3) Have you created a system to log your practices so that you can track your progress? If not, what would be the best tool for you to use?

(4) Create a list of prayer points asking God to give you revelation, knowledge, and wisdom pertaining to your specific gifting.

(5) Have you challenged yourself to accomplish more difficult things than you ever have whether musically or vocally? In which areas can you challenge yourself for growth?

BEFORE YOU GO!

If you enjoyed this book, will you take a few minutes to leave an Amazon review and share it on social media? Tag me when you do! If you hated it, forget my name and that you read it, and please never mention it to anyone . . . ever. Thanks!

ABOUT THE AUTHOR

Pastor Ted Shuttlesworth Jr. has been preaching the gospel for over two decades. Ted has been privileged to minister across the United States, as well as in other nations, with many creative miracles reported.

He and his wife, Carolyn, pastor Miracle Word Church in West Palm Beach, Florida, which they launched in 2023. They also continue to travel and hold crusades in the U.S. and other nations.

Ted is an author, weekly podcast host, and the founder of Miracle Word University—an online training resource designed to raise a new generation of leaders and equip believers for their God-given purpose.

He is a graduate of Rhema Bible College and lives in Florida with his wife, Carolyn, and their three children, Madelyn, Brooklyn, and Teddy III.

SHOP ALL BOOKS
FROM MIRACLE WORD MINISTRIES

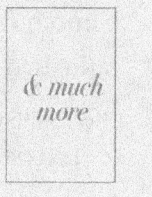

SHOP.MIRACLEWORD.COM
OR ON YOUR PREFERRED E-READER

GET STARTED WITH ANY BIBLE COURSE FOR **ONLY $69!**

Finally, affordable online Bible training courses that will build your faith as well as your knowledge of God's Word and equip you for your calling.

We'll cover subjects like Divine Healing, Pneumatology - the Person and Baptism of the Holy Spirit, Answered Prayer - Understanding how prayer works & how to receive answers, Mountain-Moving Faith & Worship Keyboard

MIRACLEWORDU.COM

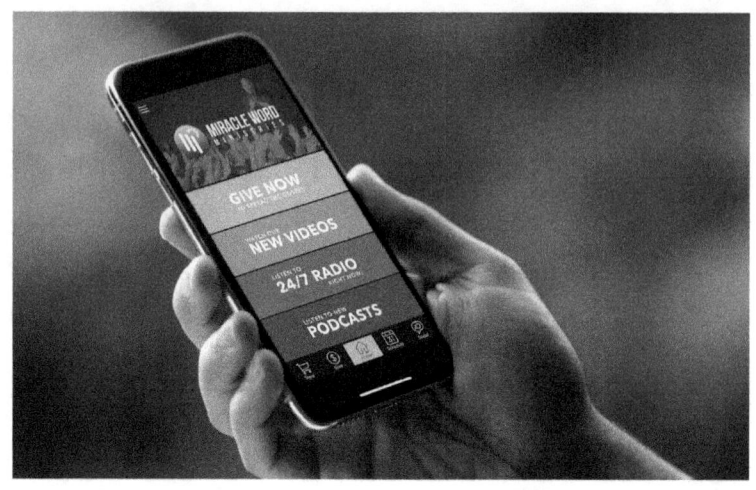

DOWNLOAD OUR FREE APP

you can hear preaching 24/7, watch our youtube videos, listen to our weekly podcasts and much more

FOLLOW US ON SOCIAL

(f) **/MIRACLEWORDMINISTRIES**

(🐦) **@TSHUTTLESWORTH**

(📷) **@TEDSHUTTLESWORTH**

(▶) **TED SHUTTLESWORTH JR.**

www.ingramcontent.com/pod-product-compliance
Lightning Source LLC
LaVergne TN
LVHW021601070426
835507LV00015B/1898